14, Brookfield Park, NW5.

THE TRENDY APE

BY

Marc

 HODDER AND STOUGHTON

In August, 1967, the rather hesitant drawing reproduced below appeared in *The Listener*. This and the strips overleaf introduced—or rather redeployed—some of the main characters from Alan Bennett's BBC series 'On the Margin'. The String-Alongs and Touch-Paceys had made their first appearance in his weekly soap opera, 'Life and Times in NW1'.

The fact that the original title had a specific geographical location possibly concealed the realisation that Alan Bennett's people, with their obsessive interest in decor, 'knocking through' and the school run, were prototypes of a distinct and possibly influential new group. Most BBC humour had exploited situation comedy at what media men call 'the lower end of the market'. 'Steptoe' had led to 'Till Death us do part'; and both had probably grown out of the need to compete with the proletarian aura of 'Coronation Street'. But within this range there had been no observation of the middle class enclave or

the pretensions and habits of the new meritocracy.

With Alan Bennett's generous agreement a weekly strip exploring this world was published in *The Listener*; and *The Trendy Ape* is a selection of the first year's output. For newcomers to the district it should perhaps be explained that the central characters, Simon and Joanna String-Along, have settled in NW1 partly because of its proximity to Fleet Street, but also because of the relative cheapness of the freeholds—they belong inevitably to a property-owning democracy. The Touch-Paceys who also live in the same crescent have remained rather shadowy figures,

though they are constantly referred and deferred to. They fulfil an important role, part touchstone, part pace-setters.

These and the subsequent figures who have been introduced (see overleaf) are unlikely figures for a strip cartoon, where the tradition is for simple if not mythological characterisation and altogether more timeless situations. This cannot be said of *Life and Times*. In fact some of the topical allusions are thought to need some explanation; and brief notes can be found at the end of the book. The reason for the vagueness of most strips is of course com-

mercial. Many of them are syndicated around the world. Flook, an honourable exception to this, only appears in five papers overseas. Feiffer's monologues travel rather better; but then perhaps the kind of American agony he explores has become an international commodity.

This strip, however, is also about rather more than the lives of a particular set. Though the language of this strip may not be the natural speech-rhythms of Swadlincote, they are certainly heard there. The upward strivers of the Communications Industry have become central figures of our time. This meritocracy has found that the heroes

who used to inhabit the gossip columns and brains trusts of the fifties are unworthy now of continuous attention: and in searching for new fodder they have held up their own flesh and blood for public scrutiny. The columns and discussion programmes of today are peopled by other strivers at the same coal-face. This book attempts to explore the way of thinking, the pressures and the home life of our own dear communicators.

August, 1968
W.14.

Marc

Dramatis Personae

Joanna and Simon String-Along are the central characters of the strip. Simon works in what he describes as 'the Communications Industry' which means writing a trendy column for a newspaper with occasional appearances on 'Late Night Line-up'. Joanna, after leaving Somerville, worked in market research. They were the first to colonise the crescent. Although some of the action takes place in the bathroom there never seems to be much sign of affection or, yes, sex. However, they get on well in spite of occasional rattiness; they seem to need each other. Joanna is probably the nastier by a rather short neck.

Moira is a television producer who lives near at hand. One of her programmes is called 'Gala Trend'. She is vaguely married, but has a walk-out with Bernard Goldblatt. She is a secret conformist.

Pilaf Trend Bender, the Yemeni-born novelist, is the nearest Joanna has to a best friend. She is separated from a conventional English husband. She travels extensively; recently she has been to a left-wing writers' conference in Cuba where she picked up some interesting items for the boutique she helped to run.

Bernard Goldblatt is the resident intellectual. He is on a sabbatical from a northern university. He considers himself a polymath, but his language owes much to Marshall McLuhan. He talks about 'democratising his talent' when trying to persuade editors that they should publish a 'serious' column by him on pop music.

Gareth is programme controller of Cumbrian Television, the company which Simon eventually joins. He describes himself as a 'trouble-shooter'. He is another immigrant from the Press, where he used to work with Simon on the feature page of a popular daily.

The Colonel formed the consortium that runs Cumbrian. He had a good war and was awarded a newspaper in one of the occupied territories for conspicuous bravery in diverting NAAFI stores. He lives in a large country house which he runs on expenses as he has three researchers working in the converted stables.

Melanie and Tristram are the String-Alongs' children. They are sitting on a pine chest acquired 'before the Portobello Road was taken over by graduate drop-outs'. Tristram is at a local Primary.

Heidi is one of the String-Alongs' constantly changing string of au pair girls. Mrs String-Along resents the fact that she eats anything at all.

THE HOME LIFE OF THE STRING-ALONGS

1. Naked Apes

Joanna darling, are you decent? I just wanted to have a word with you about the children. I think it's terribly important for them to see us naked.

We must be very casual about it, as if it was entirely natural... I must say one is grateful for our under-floor central heating.

Technology sets us free! Incidentally, how much exposure do you think is suitable? I can't find anything about it in Doctor Spock at all.

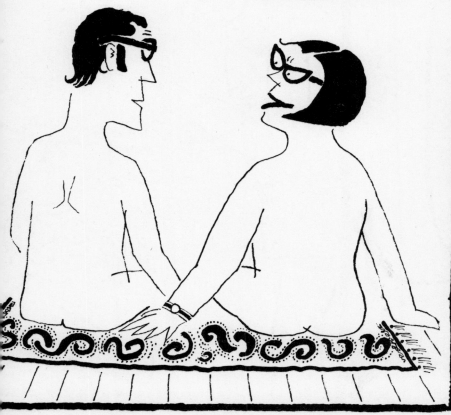

Now into bed, you lot. But what on earth have you done with those lovely pyjamas we got from Junior Gear? Mummy doesn't buy you trendy clothes just for the fun of it, you know.

They must have been watching 'Meeting Point' too often. One begins to see Mary Whitehouse's point about the influence of TV.

One only hopes he keeps Him to himself. If it gets around we're going to look pretty stupid.

2. Variations of Religious Experience

3. Mummy takes a Trip

Mummy darling,
how lovely to
see you; but
where on earth
have you been ?

I've had a lovely time touring
your local boutiques. And I've
found a lovely present that I know
you and Simon will think a hoot;
it's a suggestive door-knocker.

Skirt by Peter Saunders
as allegedly worn by
Anne, Duchess of
Rutland

Marc

4. Objets Trouvés

But they haven't taken anything of real value. Our collection of thirties objects is untouched.

It's really rather depressing; it shows so convincingly the complete lack of taste of the lower class.

REGENT

VIROL

Marc

5. Joanna's Den

Joanna's up to her
ears in ratatouille,
but she will be
on show soon.   Great!   Super!

6. Togetherness

Those unspeakable String-Alongs have had the effrontery to ask us in for a drink tonight. Apparently they have a communal project they want to air a little less publicly than on 'Late Night Line-Up'.

I'd quite like to go there once, Boysie. I feel so out of it when my hairdresser implies that he knows them better than we do.

We've had this super idea. Everybody in the crescent tears down their fences...

So we have this fantastic communal garden. As the Touch-Paceys said, we will be doing something to create our own little kibbutz.

But, Simon, why are you replacing the fence after everyone was so hooked on the idea of an open-plan garden?

I'm sorry, it's no go. I found Tristram playing with a highly unsuitable child. I discovered the father is one of the PRO's for the Greek government.

BERNARD GOLDBLATT COMES TO STAY

7. Sabbatical

Bernard Goldblatt has got a sabbatical from his northern university; he feels he's been making too much of a Hoggart of himself. He says can we put him up ?

That's a real coup, Simon, to have a genuine intellectua on tap. God, one suddenly realises how much one misses the good talk that made Somerville such a forcing house in the fifties.

Tristram darling, Daddy has asked a very clever friend to come and stay in your room, so you are going to stay with Grandpa in Wapping. Won't that be fun ?

Well, Bernard, what are you planning to do in London? Would you consider it too shaming to appear on 'Take it or Leave it'? It really would be rewarding to see you discuss intelligently the gaps in your literary knowledge.

Not at all, one really should democratise one's talent. In fact I'm planning to write a column about pop music. There's no reason why a new disc shouldn't be treated just as analytically as a pre-audio-tactile artifact like a book.

Bad news, darling. The proprietor has vetoed our plan for a 'Hindsight' team. He wants his nephew instead to write a series on 'The Birds of London Revisited'.

Well darling, that's show business. Bernard, tell Simon what you were insinuating earlier.

You should get away from the corrupting influence of your present job, Simon. Why don't you tackle something really serious, like becoming a mid-career drop-out?

You see I want to produce something really worthwhile – like an instant best-seller. In fact I've had this great idea of writing about apes as if they were people. Do you think "The Hairy Human" would be a selling title?

But who can I find to write your trendy cultural gossip column? Actually some jerk has applied for a job as the new Cyril Connolly. Perhaps you would look him over; he lives in your neck of the woods. He's called Bernard Goldblatt.

9. Bernard Protests

I'm terribly sorry to have
to desert you. I can't even
stay to hear your tapes of
Ravi Shankar; I promised to
help burn some over-successful
poems outside the Arts Council.

I do think it's
a bit much of
Bernard, going off
to some wretched
protest meeting
nobody has ever
heard of. It's
not even at the
Round House.

Look, Bernard is on the
news, holding a match to
his Gunn. I must say, it
takes someone of Bernard's
intellectual calibre to
break through from
discussion programmes to
the gritty reality of
television news.

You seemed rather pre-occupied at lunch today,
Bernard. I know it's draggy having the au pair
feeding with us; but one has to
be madly democratic if one
wants to keep them.

11. At last, the Bernard Goldblatt show

It's not because Bernard has taken my place on 'Late Night Line-up', but do you think we can tactfully suggest that he should find his own pad? Isn't that extraordinary, I was thinking just the same thing.

12. Photo Call

Joanna, a photographer is coming round this morning to take some pictures to publicise my TV show. As it's my last day under your roof I wonder if I could borrow Simon's caftan?

Yes, Simon isn't wearing it since the Arab/Israeli war: he doesn't want people to suspect him of pro-Arab sympathies.

...anna, do you
...ink I should
...k the photographer
... lunch?

The answer is 'Yes' if he's
a cockney making his way up;
but if it turns out to be
Lord Snowdon, you should
recommend the nearest pub.

While we're waiting for
our photographer to show,
Mr Goldblatt, I wonder
if we could gather some
caption-fodder?

I'm planning a Christmas
production of 'Winnie the
Pooh'. But the really
original idea is to do
it in the correct dress
of the period.

Marc

BERNARD IN A NEW MEDIUM

13. Fully Stretched

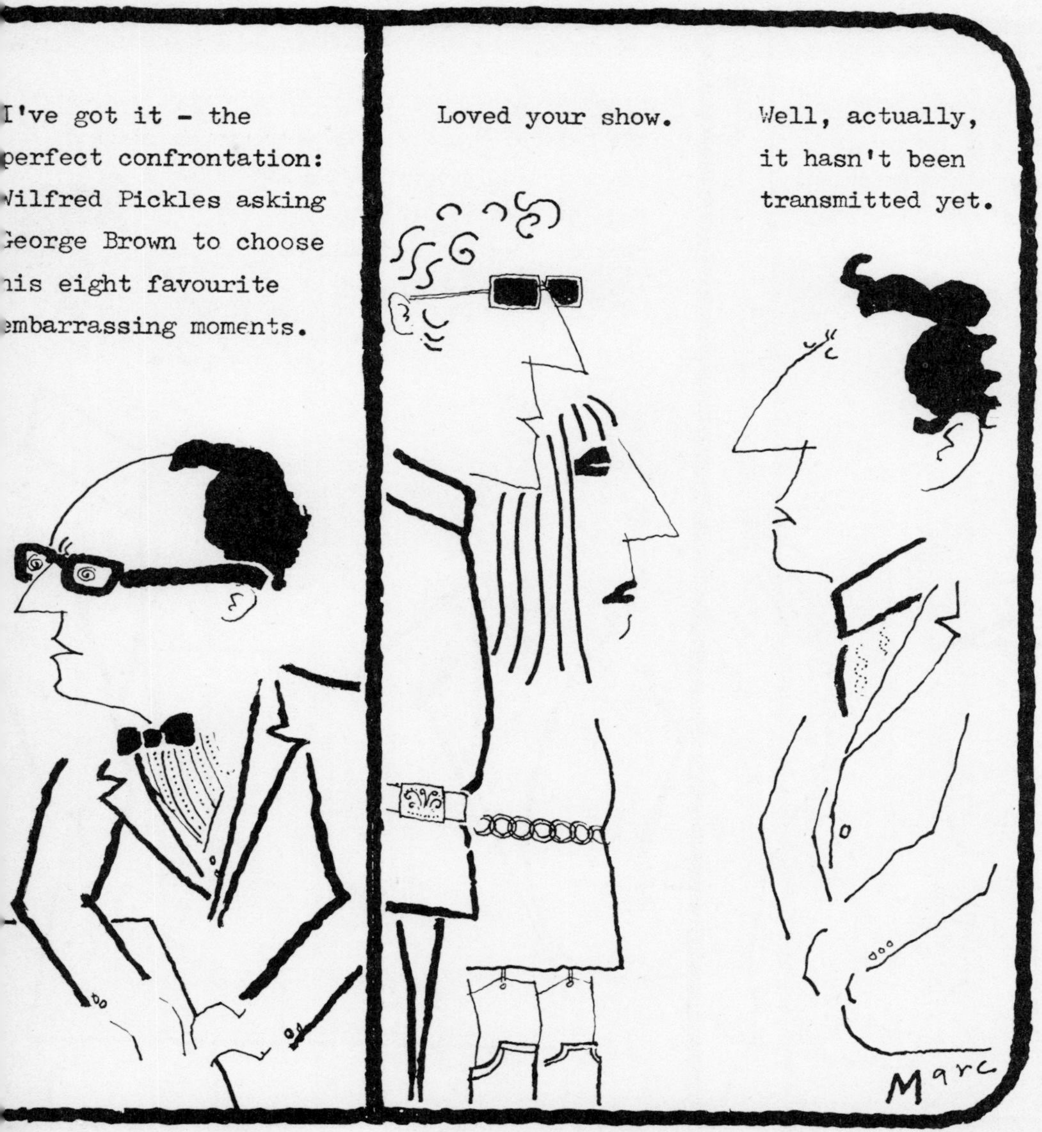

14. Joanna and Clyde

Darling, isn't it exciting! Bernard's show has been panned by the critics.

With any luck I'll soon be able to publish my profile of Bernard in our 'Where are they now?' series.

15. Arrested Development

You have a great future here; you'll undoubtedly be with me on the saluting base when the great march past takes place. But now you must help us get rid of this Goldblatt fellow.

You could always assign him to producing Sooty.

I'm certain our programme is going to be axed, Moira. The String-Alongs have already rung up to commiserate; and to cap it all I've been sent a congratulatory letter by Mrs Whitehouse.

Don't be too depressed. You know the Touch-Paceys are longing for you to help them start their book boutique.

Oh well, I must go and change into something more casual for tonight's show.

Reprieve! We've managed to fix an arrest while the show is actually on the air.

Marc

16. Pop People

They are our
kind of people,
aren't they...

They certainly put
Watteau in perspective,
if nothing else.

Hello, Bernard.
I suppose you are
doing a programme
on Lichtenstein?

No, I'm haunted by a
certain 'pas sérieux'
feeling in them; but I
might give him a plug
on 'Top of the Pops'.

17. New Heart

Now that Freddie Grisewood has finally
retired from 'Any Questions' I think
they'll call me in to transplant new
heart into the corpse of radio discussion.

You must get new people,
Bernard, to provide true
dissent rather than
ritual debate. What
about Adam Faith, Cathy
McGowan and Simon
String-Along?

I wondered if you had anything for our Christmas bring and buy-in: any stale purple hearts or outmoded second-hand clothes?

If you don't tell anyone where they came from, you can have some cardboard furniture. It's been completely superseded by these inflatable chairs.

SOCIAL LIFE IN THE CRESCENT

18. New Vicar

19. New Year Drink-in

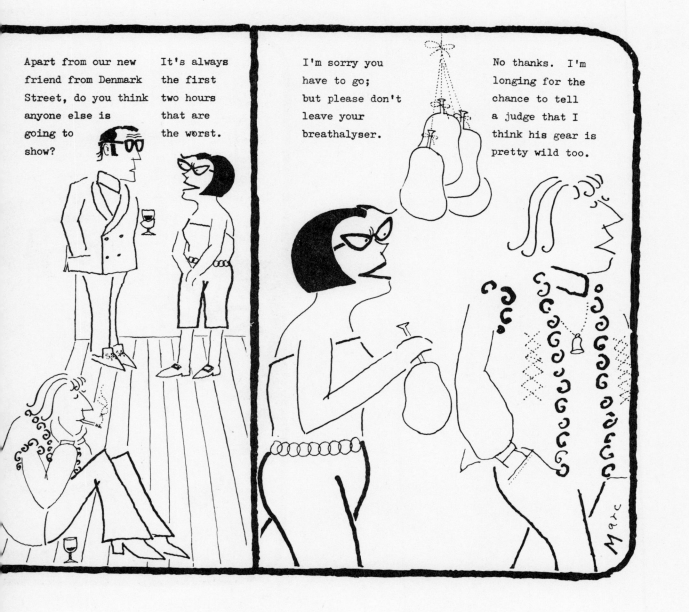

20. Pot Luck

It's Pilaf. She's asked us round for an advance sampling of some of the Great Dishes of the Uncivilised World for her new book.

Hell. I thought she was still in Marrakesh investigating pot-smoking among the fellahin.

21. UFOric

But I had no idea absolutely everybody was seeing flying saucers this summer, Bernard. Should we give a UFO-spotting party to atone?

Jumping jack flash, Simon, that's good thinking. You buy one of those UFO detectors and I'll see if I can get Mick Jagger to come; though by now he will probably be busy doing a one-act play at the National Theatre.

It's flashing. Do you think it's the author of 'Melinda', put into perpetual orbit by Mary McCarthy?

No, I'm sorry to say **that the Touch-Pacey's** have pruned their elm and you are simply getting a signal from the Post Office tower.

Relax, baby. You saw; you believed. Your childlike acceptance of a benevolent Life Force on another planet is the **vital thing.** The fact that it turns out to be Butlin's revolving caff is irrelevant.

22. Beyond our Ken

Have you heard about the latest romance? Pilaf is playing Yoko Ono to Ron Amuck, the lead singer of the Weasels.

Yes; and she's asked us to go to the opening of his first art gallery happening. Apparently he finds the dwindling world of pop music artistically constricting.

23. Match of the Day

The ball goes to Stepney, pantherish around his goal, a haunting remembrance of man's primeval past...

A long, elliptical throw to boutique-owner George Best, Autolycus and Playboy of the Western World intermingled...

To Crerand, unflagging Boswell of United's burgeoning arts...

This is just the kind of intelligent appraisal we need for our TV coverage.

How was the game, darling? Was the crowd reaction as stimulating as a riot in Grosvenor Square? How did it compare with 'Zigger-Zagger'?

Our team was in great form; though Peter Cook was badly fouled coming through the turnstile and had to go off for attention from the Press. But Freddie Ayer completely outplayed Hans Keller.

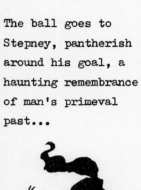
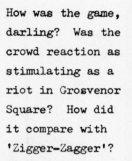

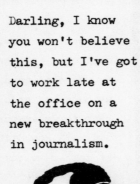

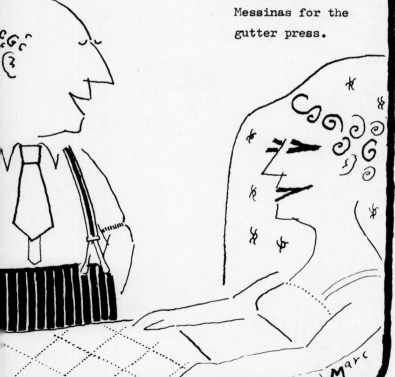

Sorry I'm late, but I've been persuading the office to follow the trend towards group journalism. I'm going to head up our new 'Hindsight' team.

How nostalgic; it reminds me of your early days when you and the boys pioneered 'Rat of the week' and exposed the Messinas for the gutter press.

THE RATE-RACE OF SIMON STRING-ALONG

24. Breakthrough

Joanna darling, I've had this great idea; we're going to form a TV consortium. Gareth wants me to be the artistic director...

If we win the contract, Simon, will we have to go and live near the new TV moguls in Dulwich ?

No, I thought we could tap the local talent. In fact we're considering giving a job to Moira; she's the 'in' producer of the month. I was going to pop across to see her; but I believe she's up north producing a regional edition for her 'Gala Trend' series.

Sun ray lamps to improve image on colour television

25. Consorting Adults

Hallo Moira. We thought you had left Big City for Sticksville.

No, I'm busy organizing a TV consortium. We should win as we've got Lord Boothby, Gilbert Ryle, Michael Denison and Dulcie Gray on our board. I'm thinking of asking you to manage our press leaks for us.

26. Drooping Meteor

I really am very depressed. My plans for a TV consortium seem to have come to a halt; and now to cap it all Jonathan Aitken hasn't included me in his book, 'The Young Meteors'.

Why don't you do a feature on the thrusting new psycho-crats. Then you could get the firm to pay for your pschoanalysis on expenses.

THE TIMES

a well-known Business Section

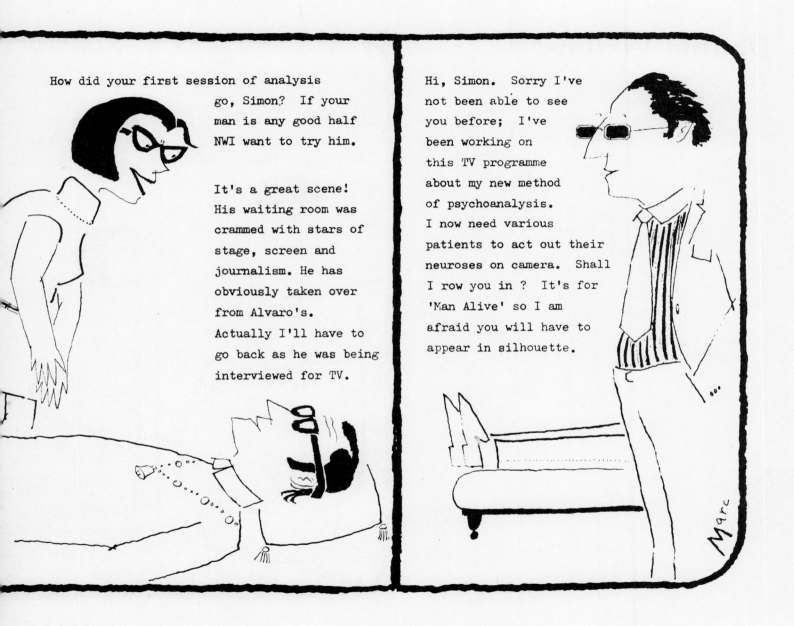

How did your first session of analysis
    go, Simon? If your
    man is any good half
    NWI want to try him.

It's a great scene!
His waiting room was
crammed with stars of
stage, screen and
journalism. He has
obviously taken over
from Alvaro's.
Actually I'll have to
go back as he was being
interviewed for TV.

Hi, Simon. Sorry I've
not been able to see
you before; I've
been working on
this TV programme
about my new method
of psychoanalysis.
I now need various
patients to act out their
neuroses on camera. Shall
I row you in ? It's for
'Man Alive' so I am
afraid you will have to
appear in silhouette.

Marc

27. Double Vision

Joanna, we must stay in this evening. I'm appearing on the box tonight in that arts programme, 'New Relapse'.

Blast, it clashes with that new series based on Alan's original series, which was based on us.

rribly sorry,
apa, I know it's
our golden
edding party,
ut we can't
ake your scene
onight...

It's a message from the Touch-Paceys;
they've been arrested. Apparently they
were caught by the breathalyser, but
they want everybody to think it's for
drugs. They want
you to go round and
bail them out.

How inconsiderate
of them; they knew
perfectly well that
this was the night
for the transmission
of my analysis of
'Bonnie and Clyde'.

PROTEST MOVEMENTS

28. Chain Re-action

Are you going to the Suffragettes' Ball to celebrate the fiftieth article published on the emancipation of women?

Yes. Would you like to come in before to be forcibly fed?

29. Through Road

Have you seen this scheme to route the Stansted extension slap through NW1 ?

What a marvellous opportuni[ty] for a really valid protest movement. Moira can do a T[V] programme; we can have a party; and the Touch-Paceys can design a protest button[s]

FIRST, CUT YOUR HOSTESS

I'm just
going up to
your den to draft
a letter to the
Times. We'll
have some genuinely
distinguished signatures
for a change. In fact
it's my great opportunity
to be listed under the
magical cross-heading
'from Professor Ayer
and others'.

Congratulations! I've just
heard at the residents'
committee that the developers
are going to make you a huge
offer for your house. They
need it for a petrol station.

Perhaps we've been rather hasty.
I was beginning to feel dubious
about aligning ourselves with
the Betjemanites against the
irresistible force of an
immovable trend.

30. Dark Stranger

Heidi, as we have a German car, Swedish furniture, Spanish rugs and Dutch courage, I think, well...

Simon is trying to say we feel we must make some over gesture to Back Britain. We ought to replace you with some poor girl from Bradfor or some such unutterable place, as our patrictic gesture for 1968.

Poor COW

THE BOOK OF THE FILM

Hallo, man. Ma
name is Emily.
Can you tell me
the test score?

Simon, I said you were mad to
advertise our modest needs - sight
unseen - in the New Statesman.

No one is more
passionately
liberal than I,
Simon.

Well, don't sack her
until after my Bow
group friends have
been in for drinks
and seen racial
integration in
action.

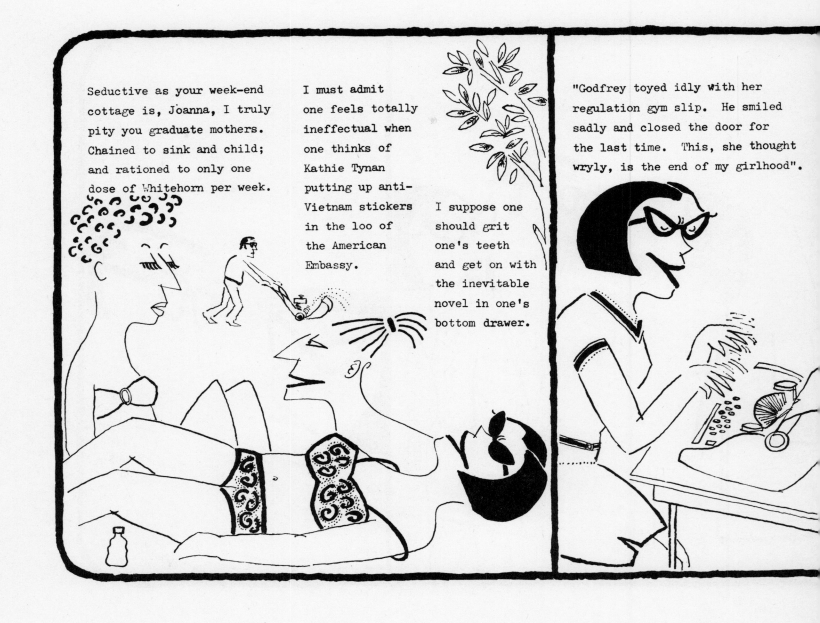

Seductive as your week-end cottage is, Joanna, I truly pity you graduate mothers. Chained to sink and child; and rationed to only one dose of Whitehorn per week.

I must admit one feels totally ineffectual when one thinks of Kathie Tynan putting up anti-Vietnam stickers in the loo of the American Embassy.

I suppose one should grit one's teeth and get on with the inevitable novel in one's bottom drawer.

"Godfrey toyed idly with her regulation gym slip. He smiled sadly and closed the door for the last time. This, she thought wryly, is the end of my girlhood".

Pilaf has this super idea: why don't I adapt my novel into a play? And as Bernard Goldblatt is a judge, I'll enter that competition for the best TV play written by a deprived housewife.

Er, is that leftover macaroni cheese I made yesterday still in the fridge?

Marc

32. Tristram le Rouge

Mummy says you must come and eat your fish fingers à la King, or she won't let you stay up for Joan Bakewell tonight.

I'm practising to be a leader of the Liberals when the young anarchists take over. So tell Joanna she must stop being a megaphone for a negative tendency in a parent-child participating democracy.

This is genuine protest, Simon. Instead of watching 'Magic Roundabout', Tristram and his friends insist on playing flics and copains in Highgate Cemetery every evening.

There's just been a news flash. Tristram and three Labour Ministers' sons have declared the school tree house Britain's first open campus of Primary Power.

Look, son, at least come down and give Cumbrian an interview.

Death to bourgeois old boy networks. And anyway I've signed an exclusive contract with the BBC.

33. School Report

Don't you think your imitation of Twiggy's Evzone-look might be construed in the crescent as sympathy for the Greek junta?

I had to cheer myself up somehow; Tristram has brought home a highly disturbing school report.

See, Joanna. Alpha in Revolutionary Studies and the Marcuse Memorial Prize for Under Tens. So couldn't I go straight up to the Anti-University?

No, Tristram; not while they say "your mind seems elswhere" in Sexual Education periods.

The Public Schools Commission have a point. Fond as we are of Tristram on alternate Saturdays, he's a true case of "boarding need".

It's the key dilemma of the Seventies. As a socialist I abominate the public schools; but as TV executive I believe in revolution from within. So perhaps one could just allow the State to pay for Tristram at Winchester.

SIMON STRING-ALONG IN THE BIG TIME

34. Fair Shares

Our brash new TV consortium needs you, String-Along, as an **image-builder**. Grow big with Cumbrian Television, the new Voice of the North.

Certainly the creative challenge of Fleet Street gossip has begun to wane for me, colonel. I'll give my boss notice tomorrow.

But laddie... Well,
budget or no, we'll
make you chief deputy
assistant of our new
special projects
department. Or what
about becoming our
Mediterranean
correspondent?

No, I'm sorry.
I've suddenly
developed this
overpowering
dislike of the
Tory press.

I think the colonel likes
my idea for a truly
radical successor to
'Three After Six'. The
Touch-Paceys, Pilaf,
Charlie Douglas-Home and
myself. Five after eleven.

If we cash
your Cumbrian
shares, Simon,
would it pay for
the sun terrace?

35. Montreux Festival

As I see it, String-Along, our main problem is to imply we are fostering Cumbrian culture without having to abandon 'Sunday Night at the Palladium'.

Well, let's hope for a stunning success at this Montreux TV Festival.

It's London on the line, colonel. They've received a letter from the ITA inquiring about the five hours a week of grand opera promised in your bid memorandum.

Disaster. The Festival committee say our Tariq Ali Protest Half-Hour is ineligible as light entertainment – it's technically inadmissible because he doesn't sing a duet on a tall stool.

Relax. I've just sold 75 episodes of 'Dr Macabre and the Magic Nymphomaniacs' to Yemeni Television.

Great. I'll go and put in for a Queen's Award for Industry straight away.

36. Cumbrian Debut

And next, as soon as a camera crew can be located, the Cumbrian Gala Inauguration Night will continue with a leading shareholder talking about her expensive jewellery.

I say, has anyone seen my harp?

This is disaster. Can we suggest it's only a technical failure organised by our rivals? Get String-Along anyway to offer highly-paid contracts to all the image-makers in Fleet Street.

I'm afraid he's marooned in Pilaf Trend-Bender's cottage in the Dordogne. He's been looking for rural protest. But he'll be back soon as I hear the pâté is running low.

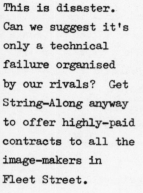

ABNORMAL SERVICE
WILL CONTINUE
SHORTLY

Thank God you are back, Simon. We badly need some ideas to refurbish our radical image.

Can we entice Prince Philip to our northern studio to be interviewed by some abrasive editors by saying that Cumbria is a re-development area?

This is a very amusing piece by Katharine Whitehorn in 'Woman's Own'.

Actually it's 'The Observer'. It's rather sad when one remembers those interviews of David Astor's about how deeply serious their colour mag was going to be.

If one's favourite paper begins to slip, I suppose the correct etiquette is to kick it under the table and say 'You can't rely on anything these days'.

If a paper like 'The Observer' can produce breakthrough features of such a radical nature, why can't Cumbrian?

I asked Katharine Whitehorn if she would do a repeat performance for television. But she snapped her handbag and moved away saying 'I say, look at that squirrel'.

I'm sure Joanna wou do it just as well. was saying old people 'pong' yea before Katharine Whitehorn.

It's really rather touching of you to
wear knickers when everyone else at the
moment is wearing those super new tights.

38. Golden Oldies

Here's another of those dynamic ideas I just toss off, String-Along. By satellite from America, the President's resignation, seen through the eyes of his wife. We call it 'The Relief of Ladybird'.

There are no seats available for New York colonel. Twenty-five assistant editors and the entire Hindsight team are already on the waiting list.

My usual sang-froid
is beginning to
desert me. Without
a Burton or a Frost
on the Cumbrian
board we're becoming
the forgotten trend-
setters of Channel 9.

We could grab the
headlines by having
a press conference on
our autumn schedule.
But we say we can't
give details as our
rivals will pinch
our breakthrough
ideas.

Wouldn't it be a good
idea if you actually
made a programme, Simon?
I'm sure Princess
Radziwill would appear
in a documentary by
Lord Snowdon, if only
you find a suitable
subject.

What about Harrowing
Contrasts of a Crescent?
There's a super old couple
across the road who look
rivetingly photogenic when
you see them silently
drinking their Bengers.
And you don't have to
say that they are
deaf and dumb.

'Peyton Place',
'Coronation
Street', 'Take
your Pick' -
Harlech have
pre-empted all
our secret
programme plans.

Don't worry,
colonel. I've
started String-
Along working
on a massive
probe into
Fleet Street's
spy mania.

Yes, Gareth, no doubt
about it. There's
obviously a high level
spy on one of the
Sundays. Have you
noticed how uncannily
they repeat exactly
what their rivals
are publishing?

You're right, Simon.
Brilliant ideas like
that Easter feature
on Houses open to
the public - that
can't be just a
coincidence.

39. **Now it can be Sold**

40. Making the Grade

Darling, something rather odd has happened: we've been asked away for the whole of the week-end.

Let me guess where. Is it Tony Snowdon's new hide-out? Or is it just an invite from the colonel for a working week-end?

Do you call this your 'think-tank', colonel, so that it qualifies as a legitimate expense for tax purposes?

I find I do my serious long-range thinking here. Which reminds me, I want to consult you about my campaign to get a knighthood. I seem to have missed it this year, in spite of my well-publicised gifts to charity.

Yes, I'm afraid you are on the wrong tack. Saturday's 'Times' suggested that the royal road to honours now is by doing well in exports. A 'K' isn't certain any more, even if you're a civil servant.

Perhaps we can do a deal with our American friends. We'll pay even more for 'Peyton Place'. And in return they will buy that appalling spy thriller Bernard Goldblatt describes as the epitome of high camp.

Marc

41. Honest to Godard

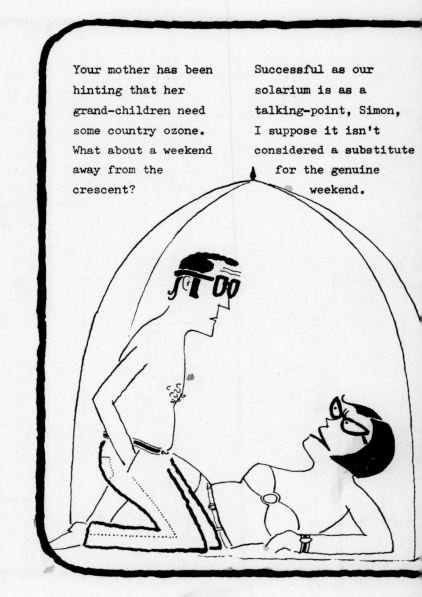

Your mother has been hinting that her grand-children need some country ozone. What about a weekend away from the crescent?

Successful as our solarium is as a talking-point, Simon, I suppose it isn't considered a substitute for the genuine weekend.

Mummy, Tristram has just dropped your handbag into something rustic.

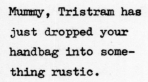

Right, that's your lot. Into the car, and we'll get back to civilisation.

I know these floods and traffic jams make super visual impact for your TV programme; but they are converting me to Godard's view of the grim weekend.

Funny you should say that. I was just wondering if we could market some Carrier-type cookery cards on cannibalism.

Frost, Muggeridge, Katie Boyle: why has everybody but Cumbrian signed the great conversationalists this autumn, String-Along? Remember my television dictum: Talk is cheap, but old films are expensive.

But colonel, only yesterday at the 19th hole you were saying that films conserved our creative energy for the real problems - like selling the commercials.

It's this new Malcolm Muggeridge show, 'The Question Why', that's really got the colonel like hopping. He says we should ask fundamental questions.

It's just a question of a crisp title, Simon. 'Which' and 'Where' are already spoken for; and I fear the BBC has made a pre-emptive strike on 'Dr Who'. But what about 'Whither'?

onight Cumbrian
resents Hugh
revor-Roper, Lulu
nd Rolf Harris in
Backchat', the new
alkathlon.

It's our great new idea
in audience participation,
Joanna. They go on for
three hours, then you have
to send in postcards
guessing what they were
    talking about.

Marc

Notes

1. Naked Apes
(Frame 2) Joanna String-Along obviously hasn't read her Doctor Spock as carefully as one would imagine. I understand from Nell Dunn that he has covered the subject of parental nudity.

2. Variations of Religious Experience
(Frame 1) R. D. Laing, a revolutionary psychologist, is the author of *The Divided Self*.

7. Sabbatical
(Frame 3) 'Take it or leave it', a TV literary panel game devised by Brigid Brophy, became compulsive viewing for NW1, though few of the leading inhabitants were invited—or dared—to appear on the programme. Instead they took great pleasure when such dignitaries as Cyril Connolly mistook an extract from William Manchester's *Death of a President* for Evelyn Waugh, or when Mary McCarthy and John Gross, who had awarded the Prix Formentor to Saul Bellow's *Hertzog*, failed to recognise it.

'Audio-tactile' is a favourite phrase of Marshall McLuhan.

9. Bernard Protests
(Frame 3) Ravi Shankar, the Indian musician, taught George Harrison the sitar. He also wrote the background music for Jonathan Miller's version of *Alice in Wonderland*.

Originally a railway shed, The Round House, the home of Centre 42, in the heart of NW1, became the traditional home for protest meetings. This strip refers to a genuine protest in October, 1967, against the Arts Council Poetry panel. It was thought that too much attention was given to successful poets, and several slim volumes were publicly burnt.

16. Pop People
Lichtenstein had a major exhibition at the Tate in January, 1968. (Frame 2) Many of his canvases are based on comic strips; and the re-working of imagery already borrowed is a clear example of the incestuous nature of the strip. The last frame makes a visual allusion to one of Lichtenstein's canvases, a classical facade called 'Temple II'.

21. UFOric
(Frames 1 and 3) 'Melinda' by Gaia Servadio was the semi-intellectual sexy read for June, 1968. It was launched with an introduction by Mary McCarthy. (Frame 2) The National Theatre had just put on a one act play by John Lennon.

22. Beyond our Ken
The Robert Fraser gallery followed up their exhibition of plastic sheep by Nick Munro with a show of John Lennon's, which consisted of charity boxes grouped in the basement. At the opening party John Lennon, assisted by Yoko Ono, let off some balloons, and in the absence of alcohol led the celebrations with Malvern water.

25. Consorting Adults

1967 was consortia time, with groups in the Communications Industry forming and reforming like fornicating amoebas, looking for a portentous chairman and at least one successful 'creative' man per consortium.

26. Drooping Meteor

(Frame 2) Alvaro's in the Kings Road became an essential eating place for whizz-kidders. It added considerably to its prestige by being ex-directory.

32. Tristram le Rouge

(Frame 1) In June, 1968, *The Observer* colour magazine featured on its cover Mr Jeremy Thorpe wearing evening dress and playing the violin. This introduced a feature on the ambitions of various people when they were children. Tristram's language ('Megaphone', 'participating democracy') owes much to the leaders of the French student revolt and Danny le Rouge in particular.

36. Cumbrian Debut

(Frame 3) Simon has returned from witnessing the French crisis on a bicycle; there was little petrol in France and one reporter, Mary Kenny of the *Evening Standard*, had completed her mission in this manner, nobly refusing lifts when offered by the lecherous French.

In May Prince Philip had appeared on a northern TV programme and was cross questioned about the role of the royal family by a group of journalists.

37. De-Briefing

In May, 1968, Katherine Whitehorn contributed an article on etiquette for the *Observer* magazine entitled 'Social bloomers and how to get out of them'. (Frame 1) Miss Whitehorn's recommendation for what to do if your pants fall down was either to kick them under the furniture, or 'if concealment is hopeless look down and say "You can't rely upon anything these days".' (Frame 2) Under the heading 'Rude noises' she suggested 'try to move away from the group you are with ("I must just find an ashtray" or "I *say* look at that squirrel!") and create diversionary noises—snap a handbag, scrape a foot'.

38. Golden Oldies

(Frame 3) Princess Radziwill, in a television remake of 'Laura', appeared in the same week as Lord Snowdon's documentary on the old. After the showing of the latter the proprietor of an hotel on the South coast complained that their residents had been asked by the film-makers to sit at separate tables and not to talk to each other.

41. Honest to Godard

(Frames 2 and 3) Jean-Luc Godard's film 'Weekend' was shown at the new ICA cinema in July, 1968. One scene showed a woman disturbed at the possible loss of her handbag in a burning car, rather than worrying about the surrounding maimed and dying. The film also showed scenes of cannibalism.

This strip was first published
in *The Listener*

Copyright © 1967/1968 I. V. Boxer
First printed in this form 1968
S B N 340 04270 2
Printed in Great Britain for Hodder & Stoughton Ltd
St Paul's House, Warwick Lane, London EC4 by
Elliott Bros & Yeoman Ltd, Speke, Liverpool.